H. DOYLE SMITH

THE
BIBLE
Is a *Single Book*

THE BIBLE IS A SINGLE BOOK
Copyright © 2024 **H. Doyle Smith**

ISBN (Paperback): 978-1-958475-70-6
ISBN (Hardback): 978-1-964494-18-0
ISBN (Ebook): 978-1-958475-71-3

Printed in the United States of America.

PROMINENT
BOOKS
EDGE

5830 E 2nd St, Ste 7000 #9983
Casper, WY 82609
USA

CONTENTS

THE BIBLE IS A SINGLE BOOK

> The Bible is a single book
> The things it says are true.
> It gives a way to make a bond
> Between the Lord and you.

MOST READERS OF the Bible believe that it is a compilation of sixty-six different books placed together with no overall plan. That is not true. The Bible is a well-organized book with a central plot that tells us about how we can cooperate with God.

It starts by telling us that Adam, wanting to be like God, knowing good and evil, decided that nakedness was evil. God, not wanting and being unwilling to have any rival, kicked Adam out of the Garden of Eden. Man then did what was right in his own eyes, and the arrogance of each insisted that what he considered right was worth fighting for. The result was chaos. God finally got fed up and destroyed all but Noah and his family. Immediately, Shem and Japheth decided that Ham was wrong and the whole cycle began again.

Now God was whatever He was. My wife is whatever she is, but I wouldn't attempt to define her. God is not definable either, but Job and his friends tried. God finally took Job aside and gave him a lecture on who had the right to decide what God was. The last four chapters of Job are the most vicious diatribe of any speech that has ever been written.

If we as humans cannot know what is right and what is wrong, how can we operate in the world of which we are a part?

Psalms says that we should recite ritual prayers. Proverbs gives little bits of wisdom. Song of Solomon says that we should simply enjoy sex. Ecclesiastes tells us that we should be cynical. Isaiah suggests that we be like Pollyanna, always looking at the best as if it would happen. Jeremiah tells us that we should be angry. Lamentations tells us that we should cry over a lost past. All the books from Psalms to Malachi give us some human idea of what it takes to cooperate with God. All are incomplete.

God, Himself in the person of His Son, came to tell us how to get past this impasse.

The first part of this resolution is the understanding that we cannot and will not suffer more than Christ Himself has already suffered. He was illegitimate; He had no place to lay His head, and He was made to suffer death in the worst possible way. Nothing we can suffer can compare to His suffering.

He asked us to feed the hungry (as in a grocery store). He asked us to clothe the naked (as in a department store.) And he asked us to be perfect, even as our father in heaven is perfect. He realized that this command was impossible. "Why call you me good. There is no one good but God." With this understanding, He ordered us to forgive our failings and those of others—not just a few times but until seventy times seven, a number that will cause us to lose count.

He tells us to love our neighbors as ourselves. With this understanding, we are encouraged to forget the "me" and think of "us." This is the lesson of the Bible.

We as humans are unwilling to look at the world in a simple way. There is little challenge in fitting into the world we live in without fighting one another, or feeling that we are better than someone else, so we add to the message of the Bible, saying that we must abolish abortion, or accept homosexuals, or any of the ways we say that people do not live up to our standards. The Bible addresses these additions. "If anyone adds to the (teachings), God will cut off his share of the tree of life and the Holy City."

This then is the message of the Bible.

GENESIS,
THE INTRODUCTION

Creation

ANY BOOK NEEDS an introduction, telling where the story is located, what the subject of the book is, and what can be expected. The Bible is no different.

It begins with a statement of faith, "In the beginning, God…" God is whatever He is. We would like to know Him, but He is beyond our capability of understanding. Some people think that God has to operate within their understanding. Muslims, for instance, say that the Trinity is heresy because God cannot be both one and three. To limit God to our understanding is a type of arrogance. When we choose to be positive about something that we have no possible way of knowing makes us look stupid. There are some who try to prove a negative and say there is no God. These persons are to be pitied.

The fact that we cannot comprehend God, however, makes no difficulty for anyone. According to the last judgment as described in Matthew, the sheep who were approved by God did not know what they were doing. Buddhists who do not believe in God, but do what they can for their neighbors in love, have no reason to fear the consequences.

"In the beginning, God created the heavens and the earth." This is important to understand. If everything we have or can know is part of the creation, we are limited to what we know, and that is what has been created. Some people choose to believe that there is proof that God exists. This idea is the equivalent of believing that you can determine who the CEO of the Lionel Company is by looking at a model train.

"The earth was without form and void." What God created was order. Before that creation, there was no possibility of projecting the future since there was no expectation that anything would be reliable. Scientists who study that order and how the world works are basing their understanding on the expectation that what has happened before will be likely to happen again. The idea that God has to operate within the confines of that order are improper, however, since the one who created that order can operate outside that order. We cannot have miracles if God is bound by science.

The next few verses talk about how God made the earth in seven "days." God of course created the earth in his own time and in his own way, but the process was orderly. An interesting note about this section is that there was no sun until the fourth day. This clearly shows that our definition of the day, which requires the sun to rise so that we can limit the day to the period between one sunset and the next, cannot possibly be God's definition of a *day*. Attempts to date the age of the earth based upon our definition of *day* are essentially efforts to make ourselves look foolish. When God finished the job, He called everything good.

Man

God created man and put him in the Garden of Eden. He gave him instructions to "be fruitful, multiply, replenish the earth, and subdue it." The first two of these are the same as the instructions he gave every creature, but the last two require man to care for the world and improve it. No other animal has shown the ability to reason about what will improve the world and make it fruitful. Man is unique in his responsibility. There was no promise of reward in this. Responsibility is part of the work of man, but no one is chosen to privilege.

This work that was assigned to man, however, wasn't enough for him. To keep a child safe, a mother has to limit his activities. The simplest way to do this is to say that unsafe acts are wrong, or evil. This use of the idea of good and evil lasts only until the child is capable of thinking for himself, but it is tempting to apply it to adults who disagree with someone.

Man decided that the work God gave him was not all that he should be doing. He wanted to be like God, knowing good and evil. Where he got this idea is immaterial. The idea, however, is a disastrous one. If I decide an action is evil, and someone else decides it is good, the disagreement causes fiction between us. If I simply say, "That's his business," there is no problem, but if I insist that I am right and he is wrong, we fight.

In Genesis, everyone did what was right in their own eyes. The friction created such turmoil that God decided to eliminate man. He decided that Noah and his family would be the only survivors, with the hope that this turmoil would stop. But Noah's sons, Shem and Japheth, decided that what Ham was doing was wrong, and the problem continued.

SOME EXAMPLES

Abraham

I have heard a story that Terah was an idol maker in Ur. His son Abram decided to play a joke on him. Taking an ax, he destroyed all of his father's completed idols except one. He placed the ax in that one's hands. When his father saw this, he was furious, saying, "Why did you destroy our livelihood?" When Abram insisted that the idol had done the damage, Terah said, "You know an idol can't do anything." Abram replied, "Why do we worship them then?"

Terah and his family were chased out of Ur when the people who worshiped these idols found that their way of living, their faith, was challenged. Moving about, they found a way to live by becoming shepherds and ended up in the land of Canaan. Knowing that the people of Canaan worshipped Moloch, a god who demanded the sacrifice of the firstborn of each family, Abram, who was now called Abraham, found a solution to the problems caused by this belief. By sacrificing a ram provided by God for his son, his son survived.

Abraham's practicality was the result of his experience, but his understanding that God was not something that didn't do anything but one who could support him in his life, made him able to live a life of faith and enjoyment.

Isaac

The children of strong, competent fathers are often denied the experiences that made their fathers strong. These children are fearful of the world around them and feel that they have no control of their lives. Isaac was such a man. Fearful that he would be harmed by the Pharaoh (he was in Egypt at the time), he introduced his wife as his sister so that the Pharaoh would not destroy him. The Pharaoh found out what he had done and chastised him.

Isaac was a weak man. His wife deceived him in many ways, even causing him to give his blessing to Jacob, rather than to the rightful son, Esau.

Jacob

Jacob's mother was a con artist, and Jacob took after her. He helped her con his father out of his brother's inheritance, but he recognized his danger and left home. He, in turn, was conned by his uncle. After working seven years to earn Rachel's hand in marriage, he was given Leah. He worked another seven years to get his choice of wives but then conned his father out of sheep by causing the sheep that were born to be multicolored, when Laban had agreed to give Jacob any sheep that weren't white. Jacob was a con artist, but God still liked him.

Joseph

The Bible often refers to the God of Abraham, Isaac, and Jacob. Each of these men was flawed in some way, but God cared about them and accepted them, just as he does each of us. But sometimes men are led to special lives that God uses to his purpose. Such a man was Joseph. It is interesting that such men do not get the same press as the incomplete persons do.

Joseph had a dream that he would rule over the family. His brothers took umbrage at this and sold him into slavery. As a slave, he was framed by Potifer's wife and sent to prison. Ultimately, the Pharaoh was introduced to Joseph, and placed him a most important position in the government.

Because he had been placed in that position, Joseph was able to save his family, and his early dream became reality.

Some people have ordinary roles in life. An auto mechanic, store clerk, or mason is called to ordinary responsibilities. Sometimes people are called to a special task, receive the training needed to accomplish that task, and find that God has placed them in the place to accomplish that task. No matter what a person has been chosen to do, he is a chosen person, for God has created him and placed him where He wants him to be.

THE CHARACTERS

Exodus through Second Kings

EVERY BOOK IS about something. The Bible is no exception, but there are many characters. There is a nation, God, and several concepts that are important and necessary to understand before we develop what the Bible is talking about.

God

God is the simplest character to deal with. "I am whatever I am." This quote is often taken as a name, but the concept it applies is essential to understanding the message in the Bible. We are made in the image of God, and my wife is whatever she is as well. I cannot describe menopause. I have never experienced it. That does not change my love for my wife, but I know there are things about her that I will never understand, and I accept that. Many people try to dictate what other people should be. When we do that, we are placing ourselves in God's place. We must accept our neighbors as they are. Often those neighbors are hard to get along with, do not behave as we would behave, and place us in difficult positions. When we accept them as they are, we can adjust ourselves to work with them.

Unfortunately, most people do not accept themselves as they are. Alcoholics think that they are in control of their liquor, and when someone tells them they are alcoholics, they become angry. Others have personal opinions of themselves that do not square with reality. If you accept them as they are, they become defensive and will not accept you. In most such cases, it is better to accept them as they are and allow them the privilege of believing whatever they choose to be.

We must accept God in the same spirit. The diatribe at the end of Job—which defines the Bibles theme—is brought on by Job and his friends trying to define and understand God. In Genesis, He is a jealous God. Elsewhere, He says that vengeance is His. In the New Testament, he is love. To understand this, we need to realize that God created us as we are and where we are. The fact that He is our creator gives Him a reason to care about us and support us, knowing full well that we are only part of His creation and not the only part.

If He has need for us to suffer, that suffering will never be more than He has suffered Himself.

The Hebrews

Most of the books from Exodus to Deuteronomy are concerned with the history of the Jewish nation.

After four hundred years, Occoquan, the Native American who saved and also nearly destroyed Jamestown, is remembered only in the name of a creek. Similarly, after four hundred years, Joseph, the Hebrew who had saved the Egyptians from a famine, was forgotten by the Egyptians. We hold the Native Americans to be outside our cultural interest now, and the Egyptians had a similar attitude toward the Hebrews. The Hebrews were in Egypt but were not Egyptian. That needed to change.

At times God intervenes in the lives of people. I know this because He has repeatedly done so in my own life, but for many people, such intervention is not necessary, so they have not experienced it. To change the situation of the Hebrews, God needed a leader. That leader was Moses.

God intervened in Moses's life. He was raised in the Pharaohs family but with his mother teaching him about his Hebrew history. When he saw a supervisor maltreating some of his people, he rashly killed the supervisor, thinking no one would know. They did know and the law was after him. He ran away to the desert and lived there for some time. After that time, God intervened directly by drawing his attention to a bush that was burning but was not consumed.

With God's help, he moved his people out of Egypt into the desert. God kept them there until all memory of Egypt was forgotten. Then He led them into what is now called Palestine.

The Rituals

In Palestine, the Hebrews were exposed to a different religion. The Baals, especially Moloch, required human sacrifice. The Hebrews had the example of Abraham in substituting animal sacrifice for human sacrifice and established rituals that set them apart from the local inhabitants. These rituals are the principle subjects of Leviticus and Numbers.

It was important for the Hebrews to separate themselves enough so that the worship of the God of Abraham, Isaac, and Jacob could take the place of the worship of the Baals, but before the time of Christ, the Romans had fought the three Punic Wars against Carthage. That war had destroyed the worship of the Baals. Now, the world no longer needed to have the separation of the Hebrews or Jews, as the worship of God was available to all. This change is the subject of the Epistle to the Hebrews, and most of the ritual laws are no longer needed.

The Law

Another part of these books is principles that are for the good of all people. The most notable of these are the Ten Commandments. Originally written in the context of the people of the time, they must be understood to be followed. The laws of the United States reflect an understanding of the principles of the Ten Commandments. Four of these laws are obscure. They imply a truth rather than say it out clearly. These are that we should worship only God, create no images, keep the Sabbath, and avoid adultery.

The need to worship only God implies that only one source of authority can be in place at any one time. Divided authority allows different opinions to be held as authoritative at the same time. We cannot allow a builder and a wrecker to be working on the same building at the same time. We cannot have people saying that this is evil while others say it is good without a fight, and fights take energy and resources that can be used for the good of all. We must accept God's right to decide what is good and what is evil. However, Christ, when asked to decide between two heirs of a decedent, said, "Who made me a judge among you?" Certain authority is given to others, such as the government. That government must be limited to what it has the authority to do, but it must be accepted and respected.

Images are permanent. Life is temporary. While we make and hold on to images, life moves on. While laws are in force and appropriate, we must obey them, but when situations change, we must be ready to change with them. To hold on to what is obsolete creates a situation that weakens our lives. We must not hang on to the past. Our legislatures are designed to allow the changes that must be made to be made clearly and understandably.

At the time and place where the Commandments were written, there were no doctors or hospitals. To be alive and well in those conditions, it was important that people not do what was likely to make them sick. Without proper rest, a body cannot recover from weariness, and the Sabbath, whether Monday or any other particular day of the week, was necessary to maintain health. Laws about drugs and health care are needed to allow people to be contributors to society, and not a drag on it.

Adultery is a breach of a promise. Our laws deal with contract law that determines what is a promise and ensures that promises are kept.

The other parts of the Ten Commandments are more understandable, as are some other laws that are not related to the rituals of the Hebrews.

A History

The Hebrews did not live in the desert forever. After a period long enough to replace all the people who had left Egypt, except Joshua and Caleb, they moved into Palestine, partially replacing the people who had lived there before.

They were not an organized people at that time. The main theme of Judges is that the people forgot God and had to have a leader who rose up to save them from their peril. Othniel was the first. Ehud was next. Sometimes the leader organized a fight, and sometimes he used treachery, as with Ehud.

Deborah was a woman who was called to lead, but she used Barak as a cover so that the weakness that was supposed to reside in a woman was overcome.

Gideon was reluctant, but finally he fought the people of Midian. Gideon was made to fight Midian in such a way that it was clear that God had put things in order. That did not keep the people from giving Gideon the respect that emotionally they felt for his leading them to victory.

There are other stories here that show that the people of Israel were just people like the rest of us. Because of an incident, the tribe of Benjamin was destroyed, but the destroyers then said, we're sorry, and tried to restore the tribe. Jephthah made a rash promise that caused him to sacrifice his daughter, so we need to be careful about what we promise.

Saul

The people decided that they needed a leader permanently. Since this was a new idea, they chose the most striking person available, Saul. Since Saul had no experience in leading, he made mistakes, the most critical of which was to anger the prophet Samuel. Saul tried to be a good king but didn't know how, so Samuel looked for someone else and with God's help chose David. Saul knew that David had been chosen, so he did what he could to deny David the throne. In doing so, he provided David with an education as to what a king should be.

To escape Saul's wrath, David spent some time with the Philistines. It is interesting to note that the Philistines drop out of the story after David becomes king, and the tactics of the Philistines become David's tactics.

David

The rest of the books of Kings deals principally with the story of the kings of Israel, telling their story without editing. These are real people and real stories told without pulling punches. The rewrite of these stories, with all the bad things removed, is in the books of First and Second Chronicles

THE PROBLEM

First Chronicles to Esther

THE CENTRAL QUESTION the Bible asks is, "If we cannot know what is right and what is wrong, how can we know what we should do next?" When Adam tried to be "like God, knowing good and evil," God chased him out of the Garden of Eden, but mankind has always tended to want to decide for himself what is right and what is wrong ever since. The problems that this causes are the subject of the next five books.

We start with the Chronicles, which are a retelling of the history of the Hebrew kings. In this version, all of the things that the author thought were bad about David and Solomon are eliminated. Bathsheba is not mentioned in Chronicles while it is an important story in Kings. Each king is mentioned, and at the end of his story, the phrase, "And he was a good (bad) king because…" The author has based his opinion of what was good or bad solely upon whether that king had obeyed the rituals that the priests had established as the ultimate good. Archeology has shown that some of the "bad" kings were good for the people, and some of the "good" kings' rules were disasters, but since the determination of what was good or bad is in the eyes of the author, we learn how these kings are rated by the author.

In Genesis, we read that God said to Abraham, "All nations on earth will bless themselves by your descendants because you have obeyed my command." In order to be a blessing to all nations, the descendants of Abraham needed to be in all nations. The king of Persia started this process. The Jews were taken to Babylon. While failing to allow God to use them as He chose, the Jews came to worship the lives they had led in Judea. Christ made it clear that divorce was not sanctioned by God, but these returning Jews required that all those who had married local wives divorce their wives, and the returning Jews separated themselves from those who had not been taken to Babylon.

The priests found the old scriptures, and these scriptures were established as the criteria for righteousness. This further reduced the impact that God could have on those who believed they were His people.

In circumstances like these, God became irrelevant, and the omission of His name from the book of Esther shows how far this process had gone.

Why?

Why do people want to decide what is good and what is evil for themselves? Mothers do it because children cannot understand why they cannot run in traffic, or do other dangerous things. It is far easier for a child to understand that he must not cross the sidewalk than to explain that he will be run over by a car. The child is not capable of such understanding.

A prolife presenter at a church was asked why he did not mention that we should encourage the mother to want the child instead of making it illegal. His reply was, "It is too hard, and besides it doesn't get people worked up."

The first of these reasons, that is too hard, is one of the main reasons we decide to call things evil. Prohibition was the easy way to eliminate alcoholism. But the easy way didn't work. Passing a law prohibiting alcohol did not stop drinking. Will Rogers once said that Baptists and bootleggers would vote dry as long as they could stagger to the polls. The Baptists were trying to eliminate alcoholism. The bootleggers were trying to increase their profits. No ism can cover all situations. Socialism and capitalism each have their good points. Socialism is needed for those people who do not have the resources to contribute to society. Capitalism is needed to encourage the people to contribute to society.

To paraphrase a comment by Pearl Buck, I would say that those of us who have seen the world understand that there is another side to everything. If it is bad, there is always the other side. If it is good, there is again the other side. When we recognize that there is another side to everything, we have no reason to hate, and where there is no hate, there can only be love.

THE HEART OF
THE MATTER

IT IS NOT surprising that Job is the oldest written book in the Bible. Job is smitten by the authority of God. All his wealth is taken away. He has lost his family and his health, and it is no surprise that he wonders who God is and why he has been treated so miserably. He and his friends sit down and try to figure it out. Each has his own idea of what God is and expounds on his personal opinion. During these conversations, Job defends himself. He knows he hasn't been unfaithful, but his friends choose to believe that he has had to have done something that offended God.

Job remains faithful, but it is not his friends that are forced to listen to the diatribe that is recorded in the last four chapters, it is Job. That diatribe has many points that allow us to understand our place with God.

"Who is this obscuring my intentions with his ignorant words."

We have many opinions about who God is, but we are unable to understand anything about God. We are his creation, but everything that we know or can know is limited to that creation. An atheist is a fool to believe that he can prove a negative. His idea that he can know that God exists can only be fantasy. We have no way of knowing anything about God. One simile that is appropriate to this idea is that we cannot know who the CEO of the

Lionel Corporation by looking at a model train. The information is not there.

"Were you there when I created the earth?"

Our scientists have been using what knowledge they have of the way that worlds work to come up with ideas of how the earth was created. This is idle curiosity. We are in the world and need to learn how to live in the present where we are. That what has happened in the past can be guarded against in the future is a pleasant idea, but our lives are lived today, and we need to face the problems of today, not be afraid of what may or may not happen.

"Have you ever in your life given orders to the morning, or sent the dew to its post?"

We are powerless to rule nature. That is God's prerogative. We can reshape the land by farming and building, but even then, we must work within the limits of the order that God has created. We must put foundations under buildings and abide by the laws of nature in our designs and plans.

"Have you visited that place where snow is stored?"

Using our knowledge of how snow is made, we have learned to understand where it comes from, but we are powerless to be there when it is made.

"Can you fasten the harness of the Pleiades?"

We are beginning to study the stars, but our short lives cannot overcome the light years of distance that need to be overcome if we are to reach even the nearest star.

"Do you go hunting prey for the lioness?"

We like to feel that we are charitable people, but too often that charity is misplaced. We provided food to Somalia and destroyed their economy. After our food was delivered free to their customers, the farmers chose not to plant, and there is more hunger than before.

The Central Question

"Do you really want to reverse My judgment, put Me in the wrong and yourself in the right?" This question is the whole theme of the Bible. Who is in charge here, God or man?

This study of Job causes us to try to answer that vital question. If we cannot decide what is right and what is wrong, and we cannot know God, how do we operate in the world we live in? That question has developed many answers.

MAN'S ANSWERS

Psalms to Malachi

THE PROBLEM OF how we should live without knowing what is good and what is evil, and not being able to define God, is a serious one, and many people have tried to solve it. Psalms looks to emotion and passivity. Proverbs looks to little bits of wisdom. Ecclesiastes uses cynicism. Song of Solomon tries sex. Isaiah gives us pie in the sky while Jeremiah obeys God but is angry about it. Each book from Psalms to Malachi has its own solution to the problem of living in a world where we do not have control of our surroundings, cannot know what is right, and cannot define God.

Psalms

Meditation rituals can be found in other religions. Buddhism has its meditation sound "oom." Others try lining out the emotional chants—the leader sings a line and the congregation repeats it. These meditations speak to our emotions. Who, feeling alone, cannot appreciate hearing, "The Lord is my Shepherd, I shall not want." Who, feeling that God has dealt harshly with him, would not cry, "Lord, do not correct me in anger." Who, feeling that he would be comforted by feeling God's presence, would not cry, "As the deer yearns for the water, so yearns my heart for thee, O God?"

We are all emotional and all need ways to express that emotion. The Psalmist has given us a way to express that emotion, and we use the psalms frequently. But life is not all emotion. We need to plant crops and do our job. These take rational thinking and require that we set our emotions aside to deal with the world we are a part of.

Proverbs

Witty sayings help us to decide what to do in particular circumstances. "Idler, go to the ant. Consider her ways and be wise. No one gives her orders, no overseer, no master, yet all through the summer, she gets her food ready and gathers her supplies at harvest time." Proverbs give us little words of wisdom.

These words of wisdom are useful when we need to change our ways, but all proverbs are limited to situations where they apply and are subject to differing interpretations. These proverbs are only a part of the answer to God's question.

Ecclesiastes

"Sheer futility, Qoheleth says. Sheer futility: everything is futile!" These words that open Ecclesiastes show that the author has no hope. This is one answer to the question of how we determine what we do. If there is no hope, then don't try. At the end of this chapter, the author acknowledges that we should respect God and keep His commandments, but he doesn't expect anything from it.

Song of Solomon

Currently, we have a society that is obsessed with sex. The Bible addresses this idea with Song of Solomon. This book recognizes that sex is important, and beautiful. The problem is that there is more to life than sex, so sex is not the answer to our determining how we should live.

Isaiah

Pollyanna was a girl who always looked on the bright side of every happening. Isaiah is similarly optimistic. The things that Isaiah discusses are ideals. Ideals are hopes that may happen eventually and are likely to happen if God has his way, but we are bound by the limits of the world we live in. While looking forward with hope, we must deal with the present with a bit of realism.

Jeremiah

While Jeremiah does everything that God tells him to do, he is angry about the consequences. His anger at what he is directed to do and the subsequent results makes his life hard. When Christ is directed to do things that result in dire consequences, He prays about it, but accepts the result. Jeremiah's attitude is counterproductive.

Lamentations

As the name implies, Lamentations is a book crying over spilled milk. There is some indication that something will be better, but the gist of the book is sadness over what has already passed. Lamenting what has happened is never productive. As one saying goes, "What's done is done, and cannot be undone."

Ezekiel and Daniel

These books introduce mysticism. The fantastic descriptions of Ezekiel and the allegories of Daniel are intended to imply more than they convey. It is an easy fantasy for someone to say that they know more than they are telling, but to live in the world, we need to recognize reality.

The Minor Prophets

Just as the books mentioned above to take one part of what we need to live in this world, so do each of the minor prophets. Hosea makes it clear that God will not abandon his people (which we now have learned includes every person who has been created), but fails to deal with the consequences of our actions. Amos makes it clear that all people should deal justly with their neighbor. Jonah points out that even if our efforts are successful, we may still not get the credit, and we should be satisfied with that.

All the books in this section of the Bible contain part of the answer to the central question, but all fall short of the mark in one way or another since they are men's ideas and not God's.

GOD'S SOLUTION
TO THE QUESTION

THE GOSPELS AND Acts are books that detail what God expects from us. His expectation is simple. We are to be what He has created us to be. A model train works well as long as it stays on the track, and we are to be free, as the train is, to do what He has made us capable of being. This requires faith that what we do will be acceptable to Him. Time and again, Christ emphasizes that God will forgive us as we forgive those who offend us. The most likely person to offend us is ourselves, and we have to forgive ourselves and accept God's forgiveness.

The most notable instance where this is spelled out is in the parable of the prodigal son. He ran off the rails and wasted his inheritance. Then he came to himself. Looking at his situation, he realistically examined it and made a move to adjust himself to that reality.

It is important to realize that he did not try to return to the situation that existed before all this happened, but to a current reality. The consequences of his mistake were not erased. Everything that the father had went to the other son since the prodigal son had already received his inheritance. The prodigal expected to be a servant in his fathers house, and the parable makes it clear that while he was a son, his future role did not return to what it was before.

Why Do We Believe That This Is God's Answer?

First, because He said so. At His baptism, He said, "This is my Son, My Beloved, my favor rest on Him." At the transfiguration, He said, "This is my Son, the beloved, He enjoys my favor. Listen to Him." Not everyone hears voices from heaven. A carpenter needs to know how wood works; a mason needs to understand stone, brick, and mortar, but not everyone is called to a special task. My own experience is that when God's voice is needed, it is a pleasant, tenor voice that speaks softly, but it is God who decides what voice is needed, and it will always be the appropriate voice. You may never hear God's voice, for God only speaks when He chooses to do so. In the passages above, he made His purpose known.

God's Son

If we have faith that God does have power to intervene in our world, the miracle of the virgin birth is easily accepted. We do not have information to question it, and only if we have the arrogance to believe that our ideas overshadow what is clearly beyond our ability to understand would we challenge what we cannot know. Both Matthew and Luke give genealogies to show that He is the son of man, but our understanding that He is God's son comes from the episode of the annunciation, and such clear statements as those quoted above.

Why Is It God's Solution?

Christs life has many instances when it is clear that He is both God and man. As God, he healed the sick, cured the lame, and raised the dead. He even was raised himself from the dead on Easter.

As man, he suffered as we do. This began when he was considered illegitimate in a world where illegitimate children were punished for their parents sin. His mother would have been divorced had not an angel appear to Joseph, telling him not to do so.

He once said. "Foxes have holes and birds of the air have nests, but the son of man has nowhere to lay his head." This tells us that he did not use his position to further His own interests and was as homeless as the poorest man among us.

When He challenged the wealthy who used God's Temple as their own bank, these people had him crucified to protect their interests, but since it was God's purpose to show us how we should react when we feel consequences from doing what God wants us to do, He did it willingly and without anger.

That He is God is clear. That He gave us His example of how to live is equally clear.

How Do We Function in a World Where We Cannot Know What Is Right and Cannot Define God?

This is the question that was posed when we looked at Job as the critical point of the Bible.

There are two particularly important parts of Matthew that address the problem of how we function. In one, Peter asks Jesus how often he should forgive wrongs. Jesus gives a number that essentially means always. Without forgiveness, we will find ourselves paralyzed and unable to do anything. We all make mistakes, and the more we try to do, the more mistakes we will make. If we accept our mistakes and move on, we can accomplish much. If we allow our mistakes to hold us hostage, our lives will be very limited.

The second vital section is the parable of the Last Judgment. Here Christ spells out what God expects of us, to clothe the naked, heal the sick, invite the stranger in, feed the hungry, etc. This parable has several aspects that cause us to think.

One, there is no restriction on payment. If a man works in a grocery store, he is feeding the hungry; in a department store, he is clothing the naked. If a man or woman becomes a nurse or doctor, he is healing the sick. We make the mistake of believing that what we do for God must be gratis, but Christ said that the laborer is worthy of his hire. So what we do for our neighbor is what matters, whether paid for or not.

Two, there is no mention of preaching to others. The incident that serves God does not require that anyone else know what you are doing, but it is what you do for your brother (all people are your brothers) that counts not what you tell him. It is notable that preaching the good news is required of all people, but that is not what is rewarded in the Last Judgment.

Third, the chosen ones did not know that they were doing what God wanted. Each asked when they had done it. The answer, "In so far as you did this to one of the least of these brothers of mine, you did it to me." Each time we support our brother in his life, we are doing it for God.

Implications

This third option implies that the Christian did what he did because he wanted to. If I give clothing to the Salvation Army, I can do it for two reasons. I can expect to receive a deduction from my income tax, or I can want to give it without a reason. The latter is the Christian way. The remainder of the Bible deals with how we can change our attitude to allow us to be part of God's world, rather than important in our own right.

We are important because God created us and gave us a calling that would allow us to contribute to His world. We are not important because we believe a certain way or are better than anyone else, or for any other reason than we are the person God created us to be, and He has given us the power to be that person.

A New Attitude

Christ told us what this new attitude should be. "Love the Lord your God with all your heart, soul, and mind, and your neighbor *as* yourself." I have emphasized the word *as* in this quote because we must first love ourselves. The woman who gave her two mites out of her poverty did not owe money to others. Quite often Christians, who owe money that they are obligated to pay, give that money to the church instead. This is a misappropriation of funds that God has given them. First, pay what you owe, then give out of the rest to others.

Self-preservation is one of the most important things that God has created. If we do not care about ourselves, we will disappear from the earth within a short time, but God has a way of providing what is needed. For fifteen years, my bank account was less than $15 at the end of each month. Part of this was because I did not need everything that many people feel is essential, but in any case, I did not have to worry for I had all I needed. God saw to that. Because I trusted, I had no fear. This attitude is frightening to those who did not have such faith. Recognizing this fear is part of our loving our neighbors as ourselves.

Treating your neighbor as yourself implies another caution. We must not treat our neighbors as ourselves as we are, but as we would be if we are in their situation. One does not give a one-hundred-dollar bill to a homeless person. To break the bill would place that person in the position of having money that every other homeless person would like to have. This makes him a target for thieves and threatens his ability to survive. This understanding helps to explain why a homeless person would spend the money as quickly as possible, so that the threat is removed. A round of drinks for all his friends makes sense in this circumstance.

We must also look at the world through the eyes of our neighbor. There is a story of a child who could see being born in a sightless village. The people had accommodated themselves to their situation, and the things that the child with vision saw and talked about frightened them so badly that they killed him. While we can often see what others are doing wrong, it is important to understand that it is not our right to correct his actions. It is God's. If you are called to point out a fault, it must be done in such a way as to enhance his worth in his own eyes and not to belittle him.

To Know Him Is to Love Him

A neighbor is a person across the street or across the world. Each climate that exists in the world has a different set of criteria for survival. If we attempt to force our ideas, based on our criteria, on those whose criteria are different, we harm them. As neighbors, we should help them instead. This we can do only if we understand what makes them tick.

The government of Haiti asked the relief agencies not to send more food relief to that country. The free food was competing with the food the farmers there needed to sell, and these farmers were not able to meet their obligations because they could not compete with free food. The charities that provided this food were not trying to destroy Haiti's economy, but the result is the same as if they were. We must also stop giving charity where charity will disrupt the lives of those whom we seek to help.

Knowledge of our neighbor is essential to loving him, and if we judge him based upon inappropriate criteria, we do not love him, but acting as only God has the right to act. We are trying to be like God, knowing good and evil. This is again the question that we have no right to ask.

TO WRAP IT UP

Romans to Revelation

ONCE WE UNDERSTAND what is required of us, we need to apply what we have learned. The last part of the Bible helps us do this. There are many points that arise when we have a change of attitude. I cannot discuss all of them, but several are of special significance.

Separation of Church and State

Separation of church and state is said to be a matter of our constitution, but the best understanding of it comes from Paul's letter to the Romans. He spells out that Christians have no need to fear the law as they have, by their attitude, already done more than the law requires. Paul says that the authorities are doing what God has appointed them to do, in his opinion, punish "wrong-doing." The role of the government in this case is limited to that. Practicality suggests that the governments role is limited to preventing what would destroy peoples peace and prosperity, doing together what we cannot do separately, and adjudicating disputes. In every case, the Christian, by his willingness to do more than the law requires, has removed any fear of government.

Accepting Differences

Paul's letter to the Corinthians details that while we are each a part of God's kingdom, we all have different roles and those roles are to be respected. He uses an analogy to the body to make it clear that we are to do our own part but not rule over others whose roles are different. We are all part of one body. "If one part is hurt, all the parts share its pain, and if one part is honored, all the parts share its joy."

Accepting Problems

Paul comments on the fact that he has a physical disability. He remarks that he has prayed to have it removed, but it was there for God's purpose, and he must accept it. This comment reminds us of Job's difficulties and the question of who can judge God's actions.

There is also the need to accept boredom. Man loves drama and activity. One of the most important understandings of the true Christian is that life is enjoyable without those things. The assurance that things will work out removes the stress of trying to be what we think is necessary for God to care for us. Accepting that He already does, makes our efforts for ourselves unnecessary.

Keeping Rituals

Many of the laws written in the first five books of the Bible are to ensure that rituals would be carried out. Hebrews dismisses these laws as unnecessary.

Seven Failures of Those Who Have Accepted the New Attitude

The Revelation of John begins with a clear warning about seven failures that have made the new attitude less valuable.

- *A warning to the Ephesians makes it clear that we can never allow our love for each other to lessen.*
- *A warning to Smyrna makes it clear that we must have faith to endure persecution by those who persecute us.*
- *A warning to Pergamum makes it clear that we must not claim to be Christians and at the same time return to practices that lessen our faith.*
- *A warning to Thyatira makes it clear that we should not be listening to false prophets whose words are not coming from the Lord.*
- *A warning to Sardis makes it clear that we must pursue our faith with vigor, not sit idle when there is work to be done.*
- *A blessing to Philadelphia makes it clear that if we continue to do what God asks of us, our lives will be blessed.*
- *And a warning to Laodicea makes it clear that we need to make our faith clear to those who cannot tell otherwise whether we are Christians or not.*

Our Future

The remainder of Revelation is an allegory of what blessings we can expect from our faith, and our assurance that we are on the right track.

The Curse

At the end of Revelation, there are these words, "For I testify unto every man that heareth the words of the prophecy of this book, if any man shall add unto these things, God shall add unto him all the plagues that are written in this book." The same curse involves those who take away from the book.

This passage appears to refer only to Revelation, but experience shows that each time something is added to the message of Christ Crucified, the curse has worked. An idea that all church members must accept the values of homosexuality has split and diminished the Episcopal Church. Each addition to the beliefs that Christians should follow has reduced the impact of Christianity.

COMPARISONS WITH OTHER RELIGIONS

Them and Us

THE JEWISH RELIGION says that the Jews are God's chosen people. This sets them apart from the rest of the world. The Christian religion says that all people are chosen. Since all people were created by God, each has been asked to do what God has created him to do, given the gifts that are needed for him to do it, and blessed by Him.

The Jews were chosen by God and given a responsibility. Abraham was told that he would be a blessing to all the world. This they have become. We have learned about God from their efforts; without that, we would still be worshiping idols and having no understanding about who God is, or why we should worship Him.

One of the Ten Commandments is that we should not have any graven images. Graven images are static and unchangeable things in a world that changes. So it is with our conceptions of ourselves. The Jews were not able to be a blessing to the whole world so long as they were confined to Palestine, so God began to disperse them, first to Babylon, and Egypt, and then to the whole world. The Jews felt that they had been given a land of their own and wanted the privilege of staying there.

No person, or people, is chosen to privilege. We are all to be used as God chooses to use us, and available to his call. When the Jews chose to claim that they were supposed to live in Palestine, they made that country their idol, and God was unable to call them to obedience.

We are required to understand that we are God's people and each of us is called to listen to Him, do what He asks, and be a blessing to the people around us. No one is called to privilege.

Me and Us

The people of the Islamic world pray five times a day. God has six billion people to care for, and it is interesting that He is supposed to pay attention to each person as he follows some humanly inspired ritual that does not help the individual or the society in which he lives. Moreover, there is an attitude that says that he must be perfect (Sharia law) and will be punished if he fails to live up to that law.

The punishment for theft in Sharia law is to have the hand cut off. A man whose hands have been cut off is no longer able to care for himself, so the law has made beggars of these people, and they are unable to contribute to society. Women who act as women have always acted, sometimes forced to be sexually active, are stoned to death under that law. Each severe punishment such as these diminishes the ability of the people God has created to do what God has created them to do.

Another aspect of the idea of me being more important than us is the stressful idea of *honor.* A man whose honor has be challenged is obligated to fight for it. This means that instead of being able to accommodate other peoples opinion of a man's reputation, the man must destroy the person, or be called a coward.

Just Us

Christianity is a practical religion. Peter said, "I truly understand that God has shown no partiality, but in every nation, anyone who fears him and does what is right is acceptable to him." This means that no one needs to defend his reputation, and only those who choose to do what harms society needs to be afraid of punishment. Because a person has chosen to do what is best for all people, to do unto others as he would have them do unto him, he has no need to fear. The law is there for the safety of society, and not a problem to those who have gone beyond what the law requires (not above the law, but beyond). God asks us to care for and support each other. As a result, all are blessed.

This is difficult. Man is not comfortable being bored and the practicality and ease that attitude provide is boring unless people become active in helping their neighbor. He wants to control his environment, and he has to accept the fact that he can't. He has to meet life as it is, and he wants to change it.

The rewards are great however. God provides what we need and the challenges of being the person He created us to be.

www.ingramcontent.com/pod-product-compliance
Lightning Source LLC
Chambersburg PA
CBHW070956120626
46546CB00004B/1641